We Shall Overcome

The Montgomery Bus Boycott

Rachel Tisdale

PowerKiDS
press™

New York

Published in 2014 by The Rosen Publishing Group
29 East 21st Street, New York, NY 10010

Produced for Rosen by Calcium Creative Ltd
Editor for Calcium Creative Ltd: Sarah Eason
US Editor: Joshua Shadowens
Designer: Paul Myerscough

Photo credits: Cover: Wikipedia: Eege Fot vum (left), USIA Photo (right). Inside: Corbis: Bettmann 21, Reuters 12; Dreamstime: Arim44 28; Getty Images: Time & Life Pictures 16–17; Library of Congress: 1, 26, Dick DeMarsico, New York World-Telegram and the Sun Newspaper Photograph Collection 18, Frances Benjamin Johnston Collection 6, The George F. Landegger Collection of Alabama Photographs in Carol M. Highsmith's America, Library of Congress, Prints and Photographs Division 11, 13, 27, Warren K. Leffler 24, Phil Stanziola, New York World-Telegram and the Sun Newspaper Photograph Collection 14, Marion S.Trikosko 19, U.S. News & World Report Magazine Photograph Collection 4, Visual Materials from the National Association for the Advancement of Colored People Records 5; Shutterstock: Auremar 23, Catwalker 7, Mesut Dogan 15, Christopher Penler 25, Trekandshoot 20; Wikimedia: Dumarest 3, 10r, Eege Fot vum 9, Warren K. Leffler, Library of Congress 22, Pete Souza 29.

Library of Congress Cataloging-in-Publication Data

Tisdale, Rachel.
The Montgomery Bus Boycott / by Rachel Tisdale.
      pages cm. — (We Shall Overcome)
Includes index.
ISBN 978-1-4777-6053-6 (library binding) — ISBN 978-1-4777-6054-3 (pbk.) —
ISBN 978-1-4777-6055-0 (6-pack)
1. Montgomery Bus Boycott, Montgomery, Ala., 1955–1956—Juvenile literature.
2. African Americans—Civil rights—Alabama—Montgomery—History—20th century—
Juvenile literature. 3. Civil rights movements—Alabama—Montgomery—History—20th
century—Juvenile literature. 4. Montgomery (Ala.)—Race relations—History—20th
century—Juvenile literature. I. Title.
F334.M79N4754 2014
323.1196'073076147—dc23
                                     2013020355

Manufactured in the United States of America

CPSIA Compliance Information: Batch #W14PK5: For Further Information contact Rosen Publishing, New York, New York at 1-800-237-9932

Contents

Slavery and Segregation

For almost 250 years in America, African Americans were forced into slavery. It was not until after the Civil War of 1861 to 1865 that slavery was made illegal and African Americans were able to move freely within white communities.

Staying Separate

Slavery had been most common in the southern American states. When it ended, many white southerners did not want African Americans to live freely among them. To deal with the problem, they figured out a way to keep white Americans and African Americans apart. This was called segregation.

Segregation laws insisted that white passengers only were allowed to use cabs, such as these in Albany, Georgia.

Members of the NAACP gathered for yearly meetings, such as this one in Atlanta, Georgia.

Legal Segregation

To make segregation possible, the southern states passed laws known as Jim Crow laws. They insisted on separate schools and housing for African Americans, and separate seating in restaurants. African Americans had to sit separately on public transport and even had to board vehicles separately.

The NAACP

The NAACP is an organization that was founded in 1909. It was formed to help African Americans fight for civil rights. The NAACP's goal was to bring about a complete end to racial discrimination, to fight for the equal protection of the law, and for the right of all Americans to vote.

Speaking Out

Over time, African Americans began to protest about their treatment. They formed an official protest group called the National Association for the Advancement of Colored People (NAACP). One of its most famous members was Rosa Parks.

Rosa Parks

Rosa Parks was born on February 4, 1913, in Tuskegee, Alabama, to parents James and Leona McCauley. When Rosa's parents separated, she went to live with her mother and grandparents on the family farm at Pine Level, Alabama.

Rosa's School

During her childhood, Rosa faced problems because of her color. Rosa attended a segregated school, and like many other African American students had to walk to the schoolhouse every day. Bus transport was provided only for white students. White pupils were educated in a well-equipped building, while African American pupils were schooled in a one-room building with little equipment.

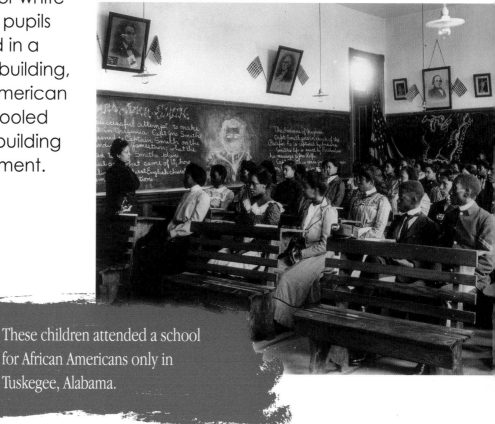

These children attended a school for African Americans only in Tuskegee, Alabama.

In 1932, at age 19, Rosa met and married her husband Raymond Parks. He was a barber and an active member of the NAACP. With Raymond's support, Rosa completed her high school degree in 1933. In 1943, she joined the Montgomery NAACP and started campaigning for civil rights.

After School

Rosa attended other segregated schools throughout the rest of her schooling. In 1929, she left school to nurse her sick grandmother and mother. Rosa did not return to her studies until 1932, when she was married. Instead, she got a job as a seamstress at a shirt factory in Montgomery, the city where she changed American history forever.

"I'd see the bus pass every day ... to me, that was a way of life; we had no choice but to accept what was the custom."
Rosa Parks, speaking about her schooldays experience.

Making a Stand

December 1, 1955, Rosa Parks climbed aboard one of Montgomery's buses and sat in one of the last spare seats allocated to African Americans. It was in the front row of the black section at the back of the bus. The white area at the front of the bus then filled up, leaving one white man still left standing. Rosa knew what would happen next.

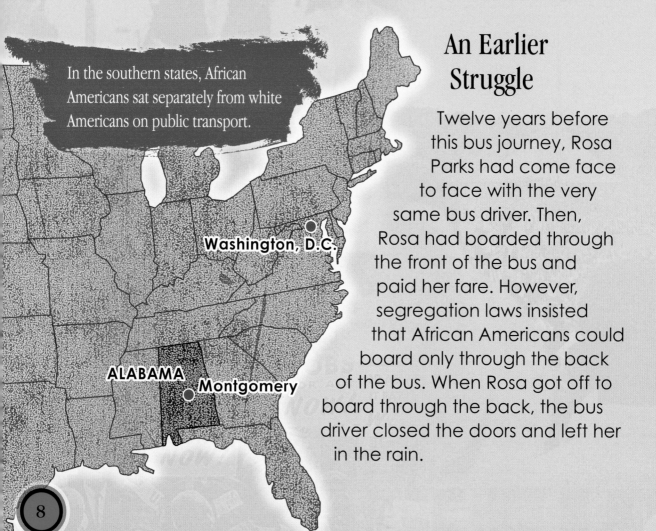

In the southern states, African Americans sat separately from white Americans on public transport.

Washington, D.C.

ALABAMA   Montgomery

An Earlier Struggle

Twelve years before this bus journey, Rosa Parks had come face to face with the very same bus driver. Then, Rosa had boarded through the front of the bus and paid her fare. However, segregation laws insisted that African Americans could board only through the back of the bus. When Rosa got off to board through the back, the bus driver closed the doors and left her in the rain.

Refusing to Back Down

Segregation laws said that African Americans and white people could not sit in the same row. On December 1, 1955, the bus driver demanded that Rosa and all the other passengers in her row give up their seats so the white passenger could sit down. The other passengers obeyed but Rosa refused. She firmly believed the segregation laws were wrong. Rosa's brave decision to make a stand ignited a protest throughout Montgomery.

This is the Montgomery city bus on which Rosa refused to give up her seat. It is now on exhibit at the Henry Ford Museum in Michigan.

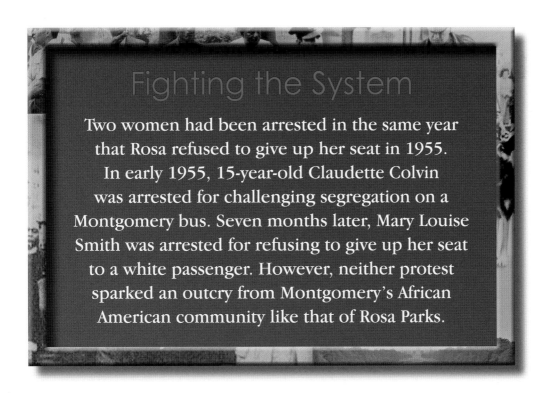

Fighting the System

Two women had been arrested in the same year that Rosa refused to give up her seat in 1955. In early 1955, 15-year-old Claudette Colvin was arrested for challenging segregation on a Montgomery bus. Seven months later, Mary Louise Smith was arrested for refusing to give up her seat to a white passenger. However, neither protest sparked an outcry from Montgomery's African American community like that of Rosa Parks.

Arrested!

The driver slammed on the brakes, and Rosa and the other passengers lurched forward in their seats. Rosa didn't want to upset the driver, but she was not prepared to back down and did not move from her seat. The driver left the bus and came back with a police officer.

Sent to Jail

The police officer arrested Rosa, then escorted her off the bus and to jail. The next day, Rosa's friends Edgar Nixon and Clifford Durr arrived at the jail and paid for her bail, so she could be released. Rosa was told she would have to appear in court a few days later.

POLICE DEPARTMENT
CITY OF MONTGOMERY

Complainant   J.F.Blake   (wm)   Date   12-1-55   19
Address   27 No.Lewis St.
Offense   Misc.
Address
                                          Phone No.
Date and Time Offense Committed   Reported By   Same as above
Place of Occurrence   In Front of Empire Theatre (On Montgomery Street)   Phone No.
                        12-1-55   6:06 pm
Person or Property Attacked
How Attacked
Person Wanted
Value of Property Stolen

                                      Value Recovered
              Details of Complaint (list, describe and give value of property stolen)

We received a call upon arrival the bus operator said he had a colored female
sitting in the white section of the bus, and would not move back.
We (Day & Mixon) also saw her.
The bus operator signed a warrant for her. Rosa Parks,(cf) 634 Cleveland Court.
Rosa Parks (cf) was charged with chapter 6 section 11 of the Montgomery City Code.

     Warrant #14254

FFENSE IS DECLARED:
DED
BY ARREST
NALLY CLEARED
(NOT CLEARED)   Officers J. D. Day
                                      D. W. Mixon

                    Division   Patrol
                                          Time 7:00 pm
                                                12-1-55

The police report of Rosa's arrest describes her as "...sitting in the white section of the bus, and would not move back."

A Plan

Edgar Nixon knew he had to make Rosa's case public in order to change segregation laws. That evening Edgar, Raymond, and Rosa put together a plan. They agreed to organize a boycott in which all African Americans in Montgomery would refuse to travel on the city's buses. They knew the bus companies would lose money because most of their passengers were African Americans. The hope was that the boycott would bring about a change in the city's transport segregation laws.

Rosa was sent to a jail cell like this one, where she spent the night before she was released on bail the next day.

Spreading the Word

Jo Ann Robinson was a member of the Women's Political Council and a supporter of Rosa's cause. She managed to print 35,000 copies of a flyer announcing the boycott on the buses. Word of the boycott spread through the flyers, local church services, and news in the *Montgomery Advertiser*. Just two days after Rosa's arrest, many African Americans were aware of the upcoming boycott.

The Boycott Begins

Monday, December 5, 1955, was the first day of the bus boycott. It was the day that Rosa Parks was to appear in court for refusing to give up her bus seat to a white person. One of the most famous leaders of the Montgomery Bus Boycott, Martin Luther King Jr., believed that 60 percent cooperation for the protest would be a success.

Gathering Support

Thousands of flyers had been distributed outside schools and pinned to bus stops. The handouts asked black people not to ride the city's buses. News of the boycott had been reported on the radio. Support for the boycott grew rapidly.

After the boycott, Rosa continued to work as an active civil rights campaigner.

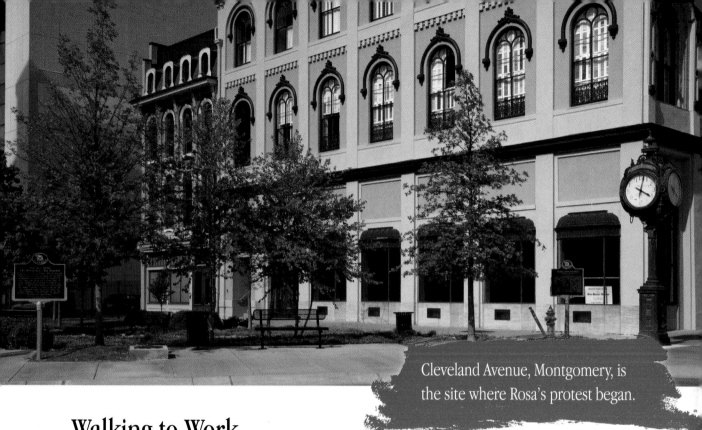

Cleveland Avenue, Montgomery, is the site where Rosa's protest began.

Walking to Work

Early on Monday morning, the streets began to fill with black workers and schoolchildren. They walked together along the sidewalks. Those who had far to travel took taxicabs or bicycled. The buses were almost empty. Ninety percent of people had stayed away! Instead, they were finding other ways of getting around the city, and the boycott was working. "A miracle had taken place," King later wrote of the event.

Daily Struggle

Unfortunately, the boycott meant hardship for many of the people fighting for their rights. Rosa lost her job as a seamstress and her husband, Raymond, lost his job, too. Life was a struggle. African Americans also faced constant threats and abuse on Montgomery's streets from white Americans.

13

Saving the Boycott

On the evening of the first day of the protest, members of the boycott met to discuss what to do next. Should they continue with the boycott and risk the dangers they faced from angry white Americans? Among those gathering was Martin Luther King Jr. "We must continue this boycott," he insisted.

Supporting the Boycott

King and other boycott supporters formed the Montgomery Improvement Association (MIA). Its purpose was to support and continue the Montgomery Bus Boycott. King was voted in as the MIA's president.

Martin Luther King Jr. (center) was the leading figure in the fight for civil rights.

Martin Luther King Jr.

Martin Luther King Jr. was born on January 15, 1929, in Atlanta, Georgia. As a child Martin Luther went to segregated schools in Georgia, graduating from high school at the age of 15. In 1954, he became pastor of the Dexter Avenue Baptist Church in Montgomery, Alabama. By this time, King was actively fighting for civil rights and was a member of the NAACP.

Fear and Determination

Despite the support of the MIA, people were still worried about continuing the boycott. They knew they might lose their jobs if they couldn't get to work, and that they might be beaten on the streets. King asked the boycott members to vote to decide if they should continue the protest. Almost everyone voted in favor of the boycott, which then continued for another 380 days.

This statue was put up in remembrance of Martin Luther King Jr. and his work for the American Civil Rights Movement.

Getting Around

During the Montgomery Bus Boycott, at least 30,000 African Americans refused to ride the buses. The streets were full of bicycles and ringing bells as protesters traveled around the city. People walked very long distances to work each day. They shared taxis and rides in cars as a means of getting around. Some white employers even transported their black employees to work themselves.

Loaning Cars

Soon, the police began punishing taxi drivers for helping the boycotters, so the MIA decided to organize a car pool. Around 300 people offered their cars to the MIA, to be used during the boycott. A parking lot was created where drivers of the vehicles could collect protesters and then transport them around the city.

Making a Difference

The police reacted quickly to the car pool and began to arrest those who were waiting for rides, accusing them of loitering. Drivers were given parking tickets, and drivers and passengers were arrested on charges of driving and riding in cars that were overloaded. Despite the difficulties, the protesters continued with the car pool. They knew they were making a difference by staying off the buses.

Losing Money

Montgomery bus companies lost up to $1,000 a day because of the boycott, which quickly began to damage the businesses of city storeowners, too. The nonviolent response from the African American protesters in Montgomery to the violence they faced soon made the protest famous. People all over the United States, and then across the world, became aware of the boycott.

Hundreds of African Americans walked to their destinations each day rather than use the city's buses.

Danger

During the 381 days of the Montgomery Bus Boycott, protesters faced threats of violence, financial hardship, and even death. Just walking to work or school was a frightening experience for many African Americans, who received both verbal and physical abuse during their daily journeys.

Threats and Bombings

Key members of the protest were targeted by white Americans who were against the boycott. Martin Luther King Jr., Rosa Parks, and Edgar Nixon were all threatened. In January 1956, King received threatening phone calls. Later that month, the homes of King and Nixon were bombed. The protesters stood firm. Even when an angry mob gathered outside his house, King spoke to them calmly and without fear.

"Be calm as I and my family are. We are not hurt and remember that if anything happens to me, there will be others to take my place."
Martin Luther King Jr.

Civil rights leaders faced many dangers during the boycott. This is the bomb damage to a hotel in which King stayed.

Facing Jail

Martin Luther King Jr. was arrested in February 1956, along with 89 other boycott leaders. They were arrested for breaking Alabama's anti-boycott laws. King was tried and convicted, and ordered to pay $500 or serve 386 days in jail. His lawyers appealed against the verdict, and King's prison sentence was suspended until an appeal hearing.

Disagreements and Difficulties

During the boycott the MIA met with Montgomery city officials many times to try to deal with their problems. However, each time the MIA's requests were not met or both sides could not agree on how to end the difficulties.

The Boycott Works

The boycott and Rosa's appeal were given a welcome boost by the US District Court, which ruled against segregation on public transport in another case known as *Bowder v. Gayle*. In this case, on June 4, 1956, the court decided that segregation of public buses was illegal. The ruling spurred on the Montgomery Bus Boycott.

> "We came to see that, in the long run, it is more honorable to walk in dignity than ride in humiliation. So … we decided to substitute tired feet for tired souls, and walk the streets of Montgomery."
> **Martin Luther King Jr.**

The decision that segregation laws on buses was illegal was made here at the US Supreme Court in Washington, D.C.

Martin Luther King Jr. and his lawyers celebrated when public transport laws were made illegal.

Celebrating Victory

On November 15, 1956, the US Supreme Court ruled that segregation laws on public transport were illegal. The boycott had worked! It took a month for the buses to return to a full service in Montgomery, without segregated seating. To celebrate the victory, Martin Luther King Jr. took a seat next to a white colleague and traveled for the first time on a desegregated bus.

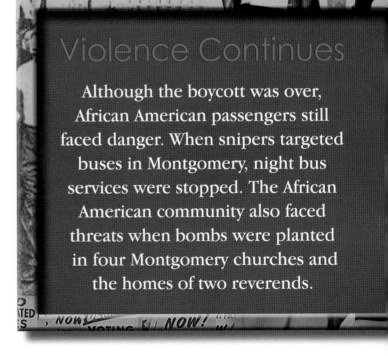

Violence Continues

Although the boycott was over, African American passengers still faced danger. When snipers targeted buses in Montgomery, night bus services were stopped. The African American community also faced threats when bombs were planted in four Montgomery churches and the homes of two reverends.

Protest Across the Country

The Montgomery Bus Boycott sparked peaceful protests all over the United States. People had seen that protesting in a nonviolent way could bring enormous results. The segregation faced in many other public places was now challenged.

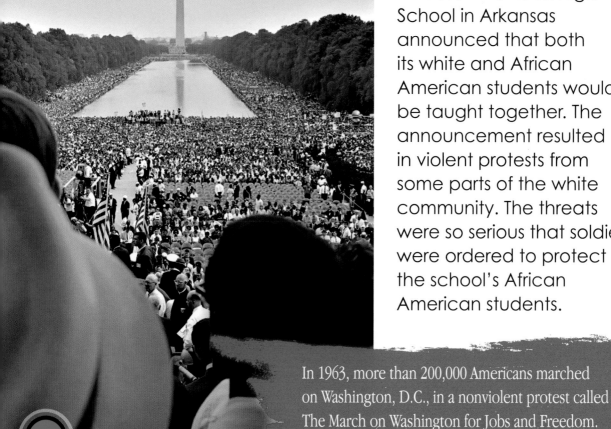

Little Rock High School

In 1957, Little Rock High School in Arkansas announced that both its white and African American students would be taught together. The announcement resulted in violent protests from some parts of the white community. The threats were so serious that soldiers were ordered to protect the school's African American students.

In 1963, more than 200,000 Americans marched on Washington, D.C., in a nonviolent protest called The March on Washington for Jobs and Freedom.

March for Jobs and Freedom

The March on Washington for Jobs and Freedom was the largest political demonstration in American history. The day was filled with entertainment, speeches, prayers, and songs. When Martin Luther King Jr. took to the stage and delivered his "I Have a Dream" speech, the crowd cheered. King ended his famous speech with the words "Free at last! Thank God Almighty, we are free at last!"

The Woolworth's Sit-In

Spurred on by the success of the Montgomery Bus Boycott, students in North Carolina decided to protest against segregated seating in restaurants. When students took seats at a "whites only" counter in the restaurant of a store called Woolworth, they were denied service. However, the students refused to move from their seats. News of their silent protest spread and it gathered support. Soon, hundreds of students were taking part in the "Woolworth's Sit-In." Five months later, their protest ended in victory when the storeowner finally agreed to serve them.

Today, all Americans are free to travel on public transport without restrictions.

The Civil Rights Act

Even after the famous march on Washington, D.C., violence in the South continued. Just two weeks after the march, a bomb exploded in the Sixteenth Baptist Church in Birmingham, Alabama. Four young girls died in the explosion, and over twenty children were injured. Much of the country was horrified by the event, which only spurred on the civil rights movement.

In 1964, Martin Luther King Jr. witnessed the signing of a Civil Rights Act that ensured equal rights for all Americans.

Without the Civil Rights Act, the inauguration of President Obama would have been impossible.

Huge Changes

Two months after the Birmingham bombing, President Kennedy was shot dead, and President Lyndon B. Johnson replaced him. Finally, on July 2, 1964, a Civil Rights Act was signed. The Act put a stop to all segregation in public places. It protected the voting rights of all Americans, too. It also made sure that everyone had the right to a job and equal education, white and African American alike.

The Struggle Continues

Despite the signing of the Act, many white Americans in the South still struggled to accept an end to segregation, and violence there continued. African Americans were still faced with poverty, poor housing, and unemployment. Race riots took place all over the country. Despite all these difficulties, civil rights groups continued with their work.

Selma to Montgomery

On March 7, 1965, another march for civil rights took place. This time, the march was from Selma, Alabama, to the steps of the state capitol building in Montgomery. About 600 people gathered to take part in the 5-day, 54-mile (86-km) journey. The aim of the march was to bring about fair voting rights for all Americans.

"Their cause must be our cause, too, because it is not just Negroes but really it is all of us, who must overcome the crippling legacy of bigotry and injustice. And we shall overcome." **President Johnson.**

Carrying the American flag, both African American and white American protesters marched through Alabama.

Attacking the Marchers

When the protesters tried to march, the police and army stopped them on Edmund Pettus Bridge and demanded that they turn back. When the marchers refused, the police and soldiers attacked them with tear gas and clubs. The event became known as Bloody Sunday. A series of marches were attempted after March 7, but it was not until March 21 that marchers finally made a successful journey to Montgomery.

Praying to March

Two days after Bloody Sunday, Martin Luther King Jr. marched to the Edmund Pettus bridge with other leaders and protesters. There he knelt and prayed to God to ask him to help the marchers, before returning to Selma. Civil rights leaders had to seek a legal ruling that prevented police from interfering with the march before it could take place safely.

Voting Rights for All

Less than five months after the Selma to Montgomery March, President Johnson signed the Voting Rights Act of 1965. The Act protected the voting rights of all Americans, both white and African American alike.

Today, Americans remember the 1965 march by gathering every year to walk once more from Selma to Montgomery.

A Lasting Legacy

In 1957, Rosa and Raymond Parks left Montgomery and moved to Detroit, where Rosa continued to campaign for civil rights. As part of her fight for rights for all African Americans, Rosa traveled the country to speak at many events.

Rosa and Raymond Parks Institute

In 1987, Rosa helped to found the Rosa and Raymond Parks Institute for Self Development. The institute runs "Pathways to Freedom" bus tours, which introduce young people to important civil rights sites throughout the country.

Remembering Rosa

In 2005, Rosa Parks died at the age of 92. In 2013, a statue of Rosa was unveiled by President Obama and placed in the US Capitol Building in Washington, D.C. Rosa is the first black woman with a full-length statue in the Capitol's National Statuary Hall, where sculptures of many famous Americans stand.

Rosa Parks is remembered in this waxwork of the civil rights campaigner at Madame Tussauds wax museum in Washington, D.C.

President Obama, the first African American President of the United States, takes a seat on the Montgomery bus on which Rosa made her stand.

First African American President

In 2009, the country saw Barack Obama become the first African American President of the United States. Americans cheered at his inauguration. This great moment in history would never have been possible had one ordinary seamstress not refused to give up her seat. This simple protest paved the road to equality for all American citizens.

A Fairer Future

Today, African Americans all over the United States are free to travel without harassment. In many ways, Rosa's struggle and those who fought with her for civil rights have paved the way for our future, the future of our children, and our children's children for generations to come.

Glossary

appeal (uh-PEEL) In law, if a court case is lost an appeal is made to hear the case at a higher court.

bigotry (BIH-guh-tree) Intolerance of any group.

boycott (BOY-kot) To refuse to use.

campaigning (kam-PAYN-ing) A series of planned actions to reach a particular goal.

car pool (KAR POOL) The sharing of automobiles to get around.

cause (CAWZ) An idea or goal that many people are interested in.

challenging (CHA-lenj-ing) To question the rightness of something.

charges (CHAR-juz) Claims that a person has done something wrong.

civil rights (SIH-vul RYTS) The rights given by a government to all its citizens.

colleague (KAH-leeg) A person who has the same job or employer as another.

communities (kuh-MYOO-nih-teez) Groups of people who live close together or have shared interests.

desegregated (dee-SEH-gruh-gayt-ed) To stop the use of separate schools and facilities for people of different races.

inauguration (ih-naw-gyuh-RAY-shun) An official ceremony at the start of a presidency.

race riots (RAYS RY-uts) Violent acts in communities that arise from racial conflict.

seamstress (SEEM-strus) Someone who sews.

segregation (seh-gruh-GAY-shun) A system to keep white Americans and African Americans apart.

snipers (SNY-purz) People who shoot at defenseless people from a hidden position.

Supreme Court (suh-PREEM KORT) The highest court in the United States.

suspended (suh-SPEND-ed) To stop for a period of time.

unveiled (un-VAYLD) To remove a cover from something.

verbal (VER-bul) Spoken words.

verdict (VER-dikt) A decision made by a judge or jury in a legal case.

witnessed (WIT-nest) To watch or be present at.

Further Reading

Linde, Barbara. *Rosa Parks*. Civil Rights Crusaders. New York: Gareth Stevens Leveled Readers, 2011.

Miller, Connie Colwell. *Rosa Parks and the Montgomery Bus Boycott*. Graphic History. Mankato, MN: Capstone Press, 2007.

Mis, Melody S. *Meet Martin Luther King Jr*. Civil Rights Leaders. New York: PowerKids Press, 2008.

Websites

Due to the changing nature of Internet links, PowerKids Press has developed an online list of websites related to the subject of this book. This site is updated regularly. Please use this link to access the list:
www.powerkidslinks.com/wso/boycot/

Index